COPYRIGHT

Nina Simone

Comic Images: Licensed Pixton Business Reseller
Writer: Michelle St. Claire
Designer: TSB Editing Services
Editor: TSB Editing Services
Publisher: May 3rd Books, Inc.

Manufactured in the U.S.A.

For information, email info@may3rdbooks.com.
Library of Congress Control Number: 221909257
ISBN paperback 9781945891779

More books from Lekti Kids...
LEKTI KIDS
TM
Kool Kreyol Collection
tm
LEKTI KIDS
AMELIA EARHART
BIOGRAPHY
In English + Kool Kreyol
LEKTI KIDS
PREZANTE
ALBERT EINSTEIN
BIOGRAPHY
In English + Kool Kreyol
LEKTI KIDS
PREZANTE
MARIE CURIE
BIOGRAPHY
In English + Kool Kreyol
LEKTI KIDS
PREZANTE
MARTIN LUTHER KING, JR.
BIOGRAPHY
In English + Kool Kreyol
LEKTI KIDS
PREZANTE
NINA SIMONE
BIOGRAPHY
In English + Kool Kreyol
The BASSEY boys
Ti gason yo BASSEY
BASSEY ST
LEKTI KIDS
In English + Kool Kreyol
Eh, by the way, tande tanpri...
We love your reviews and comments!
Ban nou yon kòmantè nan
COMMENT at facebook.com/lektikids.

LEKTI KIDS™
Enben, ki sa ki Lekti Kids™? What is it, anyway?
Well, its:
interesting…
prezante nan yon melanj Angle ak Ayisyen Kreyòl…
cool…
ak karaktè istorik, akademik, epi fiksyon…
epi fun…
fun…
fun!

Pou mama mwen

Nina Simone

jeni, mizisyen, aktivis

KÒMANSE

Bonjour, mwen se Nina Simone.

M te fèt Eunice Kathleen Waymon on February 21, 1933, in Tryon, NC.
M te renmen mizik. At 5 years old, I could sing and play the piano.
Alleluia...
Oooh...
Oooh...
My sisters and I te chante nan legliz ansanm.

M pral yon bon mizisyen yon jou.

In 1945, m te yon elèv nan Tryon Colored School in NC.
I love music.
When I was 10 years old, m te fè premye pèfòmans mwen an.
By 13 years old, I was playing music at churches...
...ak konsè nan kominote a.
She's amazing!
Beautiful music!

After I graduated Allen High School in 1950...
M te fè li, mama!
Oh-oh!
...m te ale nan Julliard School of Music in New York for the summer.
I'm finally on my way.
M te prepare ale nan Curtis Institute of Music...
1950
Dear Admissions Office at Curtis Institute of Music...
...in Philadelphia, PA in the fall.
M ap voye aplikasyon mwen an pou admisyon kòm yon elèv mizik nan otòn lan....
-Eunice Waymon

So my family and I moved to Philadelphia, PA in 1950.
Mwen reve sou vin yon elèv nan Curtis Institute.
Music....
Men, apre m te aplike...
...Curtis Institute rejected me!

Lekòl la rejte m?!
Poukisa?
Was it due to American racism?
M pral genyen viktwa.

Nan 1954, m te kòmanse jwe nan la Midtown Bar and Grill in Atlantic City, NJ.
Ooooh.
I used the stage name, Nina Simone.
Ooooh.
MIDTOWN BAR
1719 PACIFIC AVE.
First Time in Atlantic City
NINA SIMONE
New Sensation at the Piano
— PLUS —
THE ONE AND ONLY
Stan (The Man) Facey
KITCHEN OPEN ALL NIGHT
Harry Stewart, Your Host
Atlantic City Weekly
nina simone
An Atlantic City Remembrance of the Priestess of Soul

In 1959, m te ale nan New York and signed with Colpix Records!
Nina, nou pral devlope ou nan yon etwal!
I can't believe it!
M te jwe mizik…
…released singles…
NINA SIMONE
THE COLPIX SINGLES
…epi an album!
STEREO
Nina Simone
JAZZ AS PLAYED IN AN EXCLUSIVE SIDE STREET CLUB

Premye konsè m te nan Town Hall in New York City in 1959.
I loves you Porgy....
In 1961, m te marye ak Andrew Stroud.
Mwen renmen ou.
I love you, too.
Pitit fi nou an te Lisa Celeste Stroud.
Mommy, watch me do this!
We lived in Mount Vernon, New York.

Then, lè bon zanmi m yo, Lorraine Hansberry...
So, did I tell you what happened at the concert last night?
...died in 1965, m te enspire yo ekri yon chante nouvo.
Oh, Lorraine.
In 1969, it was called "To Be Young, Gifted and Black."
♪ To be young, gifted and black! ♪
Chante sa a se pou tout timoun Nwa.

I traveled the world pou jwe mizik mwen an.
Yes!
I toured Europe, South America, even Australia!

BENEFIT CONCERT
Jamaica Taylor Ltd. / Thandewye Music Corp.
presents
The Return of
Nina Simone
Saturday, Nov. 26 Live In Concert
Queen Elizabeth Theatre 7:30 p.m.
Tickets: All V.T.C., C.B.O. outlets, A.M.S. at UBC
(May be filmed for TV)
THE GREAT SHOW OF
NINA SIMONE
LIVE IN PARIS
ALBUM 2 DISQUES
NINA
SIMONE
un hommage
SAM. 22
LUN. 24
MAR. 25
AVRIL
M te ale nan la 'Merv Griffin Show'!
Byenveni, Madam. Simone.
Thank you, Merv.

M te renmen jwe mizik.
You've got to learn...
Mmm...
...to show a happy face...
...although you're full of misery...
You've got to learn...

Oh, sinnerman, where you gonna run to...
...all on that day?
Will I run to the rock?
Please hide me...
Please hide me, Lord, all on that day....

♪ Ain't got no love... ♪
♪ Then what about God? ♪
♪ Why am I alive anyway? ♪
♪ Nobody can take away... ♪
♪ I got life! ♪

Southern trees...
...bearing strange fruit...
...blood on the leaves...
...and blood at the roots...
...strange fruit hanging...

Birds flyin' high...
...you know how I feel...
...it's a new dawn...
...it's a new day...
...and i'm feelin' good...

I put a spell on you...
...'cause you're mine...
...you better stop...
...the things you do...
...I ain't lyin'..

Lè sa a, an 1991...
Let's go!
...I moved to France.
Lafrans se lakay mwen kounye a.
Later, in 1998, m te rankontre Nelson Mandela.
Hello, Nelson Mandela.
I celebrated his 80th birthday in South Africa.
Enchanté, Madame Simone.

In 2000, yo te mete m nan Grammy Hall of Fame.
I made it!

Mwen te kontinye jwe mizik.
Oh Baltimore...
...ain't it hard...
...just to live?
Oh Baltimore...
...ain't it hard just to live?

Black...
...is the color of my true love's hair...
...his face...
so soft and wonderous fair...
...the purest eyes and the strongest hands.....

But in 2002, lè m te jwe mizik nan yon konsè...
♪ I loves you, Porgy... ♪
♪ ...don't let him take me... ♪
♪ ...don't let him handle me.... ♪
...it became my last.

On April 21, 2003, m te mouri nan Carry-le-Rouet, an Frans.
My ashes te mete nan lanmè a.
But my music still lives on.
"We will shape and mold this country or it will not be molded and shaped at all anymore."
-Nina Simone
"Jazz is not just music, it's a way of life, it's a way of being, a way of thinking."
-Nina Simone.

Mwen te enfliyanse mizik ... epi m te chanje li.

FINI

Mwen te fè
yon
diferans.

may3rdbooks.com

REFERENCES

Allen, J. (2016, March 2). Nina Simone - 10 of the best. Retrieved from theguardian.com: https://www.theguardian.com/music/musicblog/2016/mar/02/nina-simone-10-of-the-best

Boscarol, M. (n.d.). The Nina Simone Database Timeline. Retrieved from boscarol.com: http://www.boscarol.com/ninasimone/pages/nina/chrono.php

Browne, D. (2018, April 10). How Nina Simone Captivated a New Generation. Retrieved from rollingstone.com: https://www.rollingstone.com/music/music-features/how-nina-simone-captivated-a-new-generation-203955/

Colpix. (n.d.). Discogs. Retrieved from Nina Simone The Colpix Singles: https://www.discogs.com/Nina-Simone-The-Colpix-Singles/release/11608730

Freyermuth, J. (2010). An analysis of the musical interpretations of Nina Simone. Retrieved from Krex.k-state.edu: https://krex.k-state.edu/dspace/handle/2097/4121

Henry, R. (2017, February 21). Past & Present: Protest Songs of Nina Simone. Retrieved from kmuw.org: https://www.kmuw.org/post/past-present-protest-songs-nina-simone

Nina Simone Project. (n.d.). Concert and Tour Programs and Posters. Retrieved from Ninasimoneproject.org: https://ninasimoneproject.org/concert-and-tour-programs-and-posters/

Overfield, A. (n.d.). ninasimone.com. Retrieved from The Official Home of Nina Simone: https://www.ninasimone.com/

Public Broadcasting Station. (2021, January 14). American Masters Nina Simone biographical timeline. Retrieved from pbs.org: https://www.pbs.org/wnet/americanmasters/nina-simone-biographical-timeline/16664/

Salamishah, T. (2012, July 2). My American Dream Sounds Like Nina Simone: The Record. Retrieved from npr.org: https://www.npr.org/sections/therecord/2012/06/26/155774842/my-american-dream-sounds-like-nina-simone

LEKTI KIDS™

Kool Kreyol Collection™

Thank you for your purchase!

Got a mobile device? We're COMING SOON with an app for that.

SUBSCRIBE at facebook.com/lektikids and we'll let you know when our interactive app is ready.

Gen Facebook? Vizite nou nan facebook.com/lektikids.

BAN NOU yon kòmantè nan Facebook, Goodreads, Amazon, oswa May3rdbooks.com.

CONTACT US for more info at info@may3rdbooks.com.

BY THE WAY, every book purchased is a book donated to a needy school in Haiti!

Nina Simone, 1933-2003

LOVE SNAIL MAIL?

May 3rd Books, Inc.

Send this order form to us and we'll invoice you!

As always, our books are available at your favorite bookstores, including Amazon and Barnes & Noble.

Send me an invoice for the books I selected below.

My name: ______________________

My address: ______________________

____

My city: ______________________

My state/province: ______________________

My country: ______________________

My postal code: ______________________

LEKTI KIDS

Kool Kreyol Collection

Check the box next to the book(s) you want:

☐ The Young Reader vol.1
VERBS

☐ The Young Reader vol.2
NOUNS

☐ The Young Reader vol.3
CONTRACTIONS

☐ The Young Reader vol.4
SIMILES/METAPHORS

☐ The Young Reader vol.5
ADVERBS/ADJECTIVES

☐ The Intermediate Reader vol.1
READING COMPREHENSION

☐ The Advanced Reader vol.1
POETRY

☐ Women of the Bible
Bible study

☐ Albert Einstein
Biography

☐ Amelia Earhart
Biography

☐ Martin Luther King, Jr.
Biography

☐ Arturo Alfonso Schomburg
Biography

☐ Nina Simone
Biography

☐ Marie Curie
Biography

☐ The Bassey boys
Graphic Novel

Mail this ORDER FORM to: May 3rd Books, Inc., 201 E. Patrick St., #3212, Frederick, MD 21701, U.S.A.

Email: info@may3rdbooks.com
Web: may3rdbooks.com

Made in the USA
Middletown, DE
21 February 2023

25335581R00027